Love Life Loss
A Roller Coaster of Poetry

Kate Swaffer

Love Life Loss
A Roller Coaster of Poetry
Volume 2: Days with Dementia

Love Life Loss – A Roller Coaster of Poetry: Volume 2 – Days with Dementia
ISBN 978 1 76041 185 5
Copyright © text Kate Swaffer 2016

First published 2016 by
GINNINDERRA PRESS
PO Box 3461 Port Adelaide 5015
www.ginninderrapress.com.au

Contents

Foreword	7
Dementia	13
Alone in a crowd	14
Star	15
My Cats	16
A broken heart	17
First flush	18
Now…	19
Don't quit	20
Searching	21
Believe	22
My imaginary friends	23
Hello	24
Friendship	25
Fear	26
Love and devotion	27
Alone	28
Loss!	29
Friends and broken hearts	30
A day of mourning	31
The only way is up	32
Music	33
Loneliness	34
Dementia and me	36
Less than human	38
Who knows?	41
Room with a view	42
Wandering and dementia	43
Punched in the face	45
Mrs Phillips and Mr Blair	46
Why?	47

Sadness	48
Balloons inside my head	49
Memory and dinner plates	50
My disappearing world	51
Lost in time	52
Solitary tears	53
Vacant dements?	54
Be nice	55
My garden	56
Think clearly	57
Go forth	58
Read a book	59
Peace	60
Truth	61
Reactions to Mr Dementia	62
Special friends	63
Letting go	64
Drowning	65
Paddling	66
Staying afloat	67
Swanning around	68
Helpless	69
Memory banking	70
Who stole my soul?	71
Helium balloons out of reach	72
The words escape me	73
Love blown over	74
Love	75
Life	76
Loss	77
Thank you	78
Love life and loss	79
The ups and downs of life	80

Foreword

The first time I met dementia, and knew it by that chilling name, was on a youth group excursion to a nursing home when I was fourteen. The shock and anguish of that day was such that it drove me to later become an aged care attendant, and then a nurse, working for a total of seven years in hospitals, nursing homes and community-based health care.

Of the many strange sights, sounds and other sensations of that first, life-shaping encounter, I recall most strongly the eyes – steely blue-grey – of a woman who sat and muttered, on endless shuffle replay, 'I can't believe it! The nerve of them, sitting there at that beautiful piano – with sandwiches! Dropping crumbs! Getting crumbs in the piano!'

There was no piano and no sandwich eater. The nursing home staff simply rolled their eyes and shrugged. Some even snickered or made jokes among themselves. At the time, I thought them heartless. Years later, after fleeing the system I had longed so deeply to change, I would at last understand. Their behaviour was a coping mechanism, for those who work in institutions of containment are as much contained and driven by their circumstances as are the formally institutionalised. They could not see, hear or otherwise sense what was for me, at fourteen, so painfully clear: the woman in the wheelchair was reciting poetry. By which I mean she was telling truths in a language that can seem anathema to logic, but which, for those willing to stay a little longer and think a little harder – as well as more loosely – can become its own logic, a finely tuned system for understanding and engaging in the scenarios of this world.

Through the poetry and by the logic of that woman with her blue-grey eyes – eyes clouded, I later learned, by cataracts behind which she must have floated like a diver with a fogged mask, uncertain of up, down or indeed whether the shapes before her were coral reefs, wheelchairs or musical instruments – 'crumbs in the piano' was a perfect metaphor for that awful place, for the absurd acts and attitudes it bred. The piano was her mind. It was all the minds of all her fellow residents – all of the lives, drives and passions contained in those more-than bodies left shoved in corners, once-loved instruments gathering dust, out of sight, out of the way of those with ears unattuned to the myriad melodies shattered and silenced by this callous way of treating human beings. That callousness was the sandwich and its crumbs – the thoughtless disrespect for the secrets in beings that may appear, at a blinkered glance, hollow boxes closed to and from the world, but which actually bear the most intricate of workings, and which can, via a gentle touch and lots of patience, still offer music, colour and truths of the kind this world most desperately needs to hear.

We need to listen. And crucially, we need to ditch the sandwich – I mean the widespread disrespect and disregard not only for the elderly but for all who shatter or strain the hegemonically defined moulds our society problematically equates with youth, health, mental capacity and thus valid personhood. In its current state and with our current ways of doing things, Australian society is a piano filled with crumbs, a system in which nearly all the keys stick. Of the many systems within this system, our health care must be among the crumbiest – by which I mean poorly funded, yes, but also riddled with attitudes and practices presently demanding overhauls. However, as my failed career taught me, such overhauls cannot be enacted by any one individual, and probably can't succeed if attempted purely within health care without address to the bigger picture: small and momentary changes can happen this way, yes, but protocol tends to thwart or redirect any attempt at broad-scale shifts; over the course of exhausting years, those who attempt to change the system are usually, in small to large ways, changed by it (or else we quit). What is needed is a complete revision of the cultures that drive health care protocols. These cultures include, I believe, not only those of health care, but all those collectively forming that formidable beast known and unknown as Australian Culture. We must dismantle the normative delusions that are the veins and sinews of that beast (for instance, the deluded belief that a silent piano contains no strings and offers no music, that a person with dementia should be shut away, that they have nothing left to offer).

Thank goodness, then, for Kate Swaffer's new poetry collection, which signals all the grim issues I have just described, and which – unlike the bleak-if-true portrait I have just painted – does so with humour, light and optimism. For these are poems about more than just 'days with dementia'. They are poems, as the title signals, about love and life brought to focus through loss. They are the poems of a woman who has lived, and lives, a rich roller coaster of experiences. Kate is another former nurse, keenly aware of the health care system and its need for change. She is also a published author and an academic who holds a Master of Science and recently commenced a PhD. Furthermore, she is a disability rights activist, a mother, friend, traveller, cat lover, social butterfly, and someone who, in the midst of study, work and living life to the hilt, received the shock diagnosis of younger-onset dementia. As Kate's poems detail, this news changed her life. But not as her first doctors predicted. Instead of retreating into a shell of seeming nothingness, Kate has forged strategies for living with dementia and indeed for living well (albeit not without major effort on Kate's part as well as support from her husband, sons and close friends). Better still, she has become a role model and an advocate, demonstrating for others that life and love *with* (not *after*) dementia is possible, that the losses, though painful, can entail new discoveries and pleasures, that there are alternatives to the grim scenario I earlier described.

Kate's book adds to this ongoing project of living and demonstrating how it is possible to live. Yet the book is simultaneously quite simply a striking artistic achievement in its own right, brimming with delicious imagery, formal invention, linguistic play and philosophical insights relevant to all of us who live and love and sometimes lose – dementia or no dementia. The creativity and honed precision of the poems is a feat of poetic prowess over which any writer would hold gloating rights. Knowing the circumstances of the book's composition makes this feat even more remarkable. Kate's poems become beacons and reminders that people living with dementia can exercise prolific creativity, indeed cleverness. They can philosophise and invent, have endless gifts to offer. Furthermore, there are perhaps certain gifts that only people living with dementia can offer – gifts that a broad social failure to listen has led to us missing out on, and missing out big time. Kate's gifts are the insights her hard road has won her. For as her poems 'Sadness' and 'Loss' so perfectly relate, hardships are creators of beauty, are teachers that open us to growth, healing and meaning, to new conceptions of life's preciousness. This preciousness shines throughout the collection in which a recurrent theme – whether stated directly, as in 'Room With a View' and 'The Ups and Downs of Life', or in more subtle ways, as in 'My Garden', 'Peace' and 'Thank You' – is that of being lucky, grateful and glad to be alive.

Kate's poetic expressions of gladness are, in my view, acts

of glorious defiance, even activism. For Kate dares to declare gladness in the face of predictions all gladness would fade; she finds and creates the very possibility and possibilities our outmoded medical models deem impossible. Kate's book solicits a clear call for change, and ought to be required reading for all working in health care – indeed for anybody likely to ever encounter any person with dementia in any situation whatsoever, which effectively means it should be required reading full stop. Through dips into valleys of loss, this poetic roller coaster reminds us why we love. It takes us through lows that don't just punctuate the highs, but make them possible, bringing new appreciation for the giddying ride that is life. Unexpected turns, loops and corners make it a rocky ride, yes, but worth it. Hang on and enjoy.

Amelia Walker PhD

Dementia

Daring
Engaging
Meaningful
Everlasting
New friends
Terminal
Insight
Absolute

Alone in a crowd

Caught behind the apostles of life
Strapped in by a sea of moving limbs
And throbbing hearts

Clambering for pole position
Each and every one
Yearning for the ribbon

The ribbon of a good life
Messages not heard
Samples of life passing by

Fanciful wondrous dreaming
Of yesterdays long gone
And tomorrows still to come

But what of the now
Still part of the mob
Alone in a crowd

Star

My Russian Blue cat
The most wonderful friend
Our beautiful loving companion

Unwell beyond words
Leukaemia or a lymphoma
Even though some of the time

She doesn't look or act sick
We won't stop caring for her
Or believing her

We'll nurse her until the very end
No doubts, no words defying the vet
With the option of a legal release

From all pain and suffering
So much more humane for animals
Than for our beloved humans

My Cats

Star now gone to the place where sleeping cats go
Boris still looking for her, everywhere
Facing the loneliness, lost from his playfulness
Yearning for his playmate

Missing the cat dance they played together at night
The daytime antics, the lizards brought inside
Which she watched him torment
Until I saved it from their games

She mothered him and bossed him
But they were together more than we were
House sitting, staving off the burglars
As they slept on our bed for most of the day

And then me, grieving for my cat
Missing the plush softness of fur
The contented purring
Soothing the symptoms of dementia

A broken heart

Love…the focus of our hearts
The reason for our being
And joy in our day
A look a gentle touch

Or the pain in our heart
So broken when love is lost
Philosophy and reason
Neither heals the pain

Only time slows the hurt
But that small place in our heart
Will always hurt
It will feel the love of those lost

Forever broken hearted
The more we loved
The more we hurt
The longer it takes to move on

First flush

Like new love
The first roses
Seem the sweetest

That first flush
Of colour and scent
Matching the twang

Our heartstrings
Beating frantically
With new love

Rapturously circling
Our brain and heart
With wonder

Now...

Wondering why yesterday and tomorrow
Lurk in the recesses of our mind
Stalking, daring, trying to push
Today into oblivion

Every day of waking up
A gift of life love and loss
Integral parts
Of the rich pageant

Every single day
Today, right now
A gift more beautiful
Than any other

Don't quit

When your destination seems out of reach
Sit down and look behind you
You will have come a long way

Wherever you might sit right now
Once seemed out of reach
It is the making of beautiful tomorrows

Searching

Searching through the recesses of my mind
Silently stalking the inside of my heart
My mind adrift with questions

Deep pondering on the meaning of life
The reason why we exist at all
God no longer a definitive for me

Existence bearing down on thinking
My brain spinning like a top
Too many thoughts to speak out loud

As the colouring of my world is changed forever
Poetry and stories spurting forth like a fountain
Like an artist with an iPad or palette and brush

Gone forever
The search for meaning
On this wonderful ride called life

Believe

Believe in yourself and your life
Believe you can do anything you set your mind to
Even if in reality you can't pick up that aeroplane

Believe you can when others say you can't
Believe your children can even when they think they can't
Especially when you think they can't

Believe in more than the negative
Believe that you can reach the stars of your dreams
And the goals of your life

Believe there is life after dementia
Believe the diagnosis is not the end
Even when others say it is

Believe in today and tomorrow
Believe that love will get you through
And it will…

My imaginary friends

BethyB and Shibley
Friendly and fanciful chats online
Discovered through our blogs
Pulled together by a shared passion
A dream to improve dementia care

Plans for a lunch meeting
Honoured they have made such an effort to meet
Sons will be thrilled they are real and not axe murderers
One husband put in his place as we are real!

No imaginary friends in this wonderful lot
Just loads more to meet and tweet
January 2014 on some of their calendars
Already tempting us to do it again

Reigniting a dream to meet all of my online friends
Vanessa in France, VK in the USA
Bonds of friendship
Reaching past the stars

Hello

Hello it is nice to meet you
My online friends
And lovely to chat to those I've met for real
Admonished for meeting up with strangers

Not even Skype or the telephone
To check they are not imaginary
Perhaps even axe murderers or paedophiles
A poor example of safety to the children

So come on Twitter
Keep me on the straight and narrow
Send me back to the telephone
Or at least Skype so I can see my predators

Before I say hello!

Friendship

Weekends full of friends
Friendship filling the hallways
With laughter love and kinship
That outweighs forgetfulness

Photographs of days gone by
Of children all grown up
Nappies teething rings and toddlers
Transformed by the years

Into brilliant young men and women
Fulfilling their own dreams and spaces
Reminding us we are getting old
Laughter transforming our hearts

Filling our souls with love
The ghosts of our youth
Hidden by the wisdom of those stories
Gently moving us into maturity

Like a good red wine or an old red rose
Beauty abundantly residing within
The arteries of our hearts

Fear

Fear hiding inside our heart
Facing us to look within
To search for new ways of being

Fear instilled its ugly self
Right back alongside our soul
Taunting us to give in to it

Fear put back in its place
Rising above dementia
With love and laughter
A new day born rejecting fear

Love and devotion

Burning brightly inside my heart
Gently holds the strings together
Protecting them from despair
Sparkling like glow worms

Small dots glowing in the night
Warming my bloody veins
Filling them with patience
Fired up to face anything

Any blip on the human horizon
Wherever it comes from
No match for the
Love inside my heart

Alone

Alone
In a crowded room
An isolated hallway
Inside a dementia ward

Alone
He sat staring out through the window
Hoping for glimpses of humanity
Praying it would all end

Alone
Leaving the other residents he slid down the wall
Wishing for peace and comfort
Desperation inside his heart

All alone

Loss!

Tragedy so great
Illuminating you with sadness
Seems impossible to recover

Lack of lustre lasting forever
Acceptance and healing
A lifetime away

To hear a song or smell a scent
That throws you right back
Into the pit of grief

One step forward
Many steps backwards
From the intensity of sorrow

Meaninglessness, emptiness
Impaired judgements
Damaged relationships

Memories stained with pain
Walls crumbling inside your heart
The journey of loss is long

Friends and broken hearts

The bonds of friendship waver tenderly in the wind
People who come into our lives for a reason, a season or a lifetime
Never knowing which one they will be, or which one we will be
Waiting in the wings to share our dreams, our lives, our losses

Stepping in when they see us falling or hurting
Jumping high for joy with us when we celebrate
Never doubting us

Wanting to spend time in the arms and hearts of each other
Knowing when to back off, when to come closer
Nearby in times of grief, even when there are no words
A hug, a kiss, a healing glance, somewhere to land a broken heart

When there are no songs or conversations
They stay comfortingly close by with friendship and love
To help you mend a broken heart

A day of mourning

Milestones on the road to death
Every cell of the body starting to fade
And yet the human spirit prevails
The heart throbbing defiantly in spite of dementia

One whole week struggling against another setback
A life well lived, but trying to hold on
His incredible intellect and humour
Wanting to let go, not quite knowing how

Trying to protect us all from the pain of his death
The reality and starkness of life without him
We will miss you my friend…
Rest in peace Michael John Stone

The only way is up

A room full of hearts
Opened wide with hope
Holding hands

Supporting each other
Feeling less alone
Sharing struggles and stepping stones

Wondering if fading capacities will matter
Finding new ways
What we can't do alone

We can to together
The road ahead a new one
See you at the top

Music

Wafting along corridors
Into the alcove of our mind
Awakening the soul

Memories stirred
Thoughts of yesterdays
And long lost loves

Visions rekindled
Childhoods and playgrounds
Tucked inside schoolyards

Teachers and yard duty
Old boyfriends and love letters
Tattooed with red lipstick kisses

Whispering to heart heartstrings
Rekindled moments lost in time
Healing all wounds

Loneliness

Loneliness sits silently
Too often tinged with sadness
Wafting through one's heart
Waiting for no one in particular

Filling one's soul with curiosity
Wondering why
It never quite goes away
A movie or a book

Beautiful music
Amongst a pulsing crowd
Or all alone
There is no difference

When loneliness and sadness
Sneaks in
Nothing takes it away
Not quite ever

The memory of old grief
Maybe a suicide or divorce
Always a death of some kind
Intertwined with new losses

Dementia and aloneness
Too hard to describe
With spoken words
But through poetry

Highlighting
Those wretched feelings
Of loneliness and sadness
Deep inside one's heart

Dementia and me

What the hell happened to my brain
Diagnosed with dementia when I was much too young
My children still at school
A deadly terminal disease effecting
Memory, thinking, perception, judgment, language and speech
But worse than that, affecting my
Life, family, friendships, my sense of self, my identity
And a bucket full of guilt
Truckloads of stigma discrimination and isolation
Loss of dreams, and grief
Sadness, disbelief, lost employment
And yet a new purpose of advocacy and activism
To bring about change
To stop the blatant abuse of the most basic of human rights
Of people diagnosed with dementia, young or old
Fewer old friends, new global friendships
The role of educator
Teaching global lessons to academics and carers
Hoping for and seeking change
Searching for new ways for professionals
To discover we deserve the same as others with illness
Not involuntary restraint
Eventually locked away in secure memory units
Given drugs or using physical restraints to make us compliant
The justification it's for our safety
Helping aged care and hospitals comply with their duty of care
Avoiding insurance claims
Worse than being locked in prison
The person with dementia
Has not broken the law or done anything wrong

They are not criminals
They have a degenerative cognitive disease
Needing love and care
We need support to remain engaged with pre-diagnosis activities
Counselling to stay motivated
A disAbility access plan and assisted technologies
DisAbility equipment, mentoring
Positive psychology for our sense of well being
Above all other things
To be treated with dignity as whole human beings

Less than human

A week full of head spins
On Monday a visit to the neurologist
The results of the latest SPECT scan
And the neuropsychology tests…
Bad news

The dementia has progressed clinically
My frontal lobes are now involved
Yet still I am not presenting as poorly
As the clinical picture indicates…
Good news

I wonder what this really means
Am I having more irrational thoughts?
Making bad decisions
Perhaps yesterday has proven
This is so

Standing on a swivel chair
Reaching up to a high cupboard
Then spinning uncontrollably
Bouncing with the force of the spinning
Whack

Head elbow hip crashing onto bookcase
Yelping for help as I thumped
A crumpled heap on the floor
No signs of recall later
Out cold

Waking to the sounds of Jodi
Calling an ambulance
Strapped into a neck brace
Heading to a private hospital
Oh no

To be treated like a moron
Simply because of three words
'She has dementia'
The first nurse asked me would I cooperate…
Or would they have to sedate me!

And at shift handover I was referred to as Bay 18
Then they talked about me
Not to me
At the mention of dementia, one nurse asked the other
Was I able to speak, would I be cooperative?
I raised the nerve to rise above their insults
And suggested they ask me
Even as my head continued to hurt and spin
No wonder the research clearly shows
People with dementia do not do well in hospitals

Staff not trained to know how to treat them
Even though they are a 'caring' profession
Following a CT scan of my head and neck
And a few hours of observation
I went home with no serious injury other than insults

An egg on my head, a black elbow
A few other aches and bruises
I feel like I've been in a car crash
Stiff, bruised a headache and aching body parts
But most of all deeply annoyed

To be reminded once again
People with dementia
Are somehow
Seen to be
Less than human

Who knows?

He knows what he knows
And she knows what she knows
But who knows what she knows
And who knows what he knows

Some days I don't know
What I know
Let alone what he knows
And even less what she knows

It's a strange conundrum
Wondering what he knows
Or she knows
When most days

I've got trouble
Remembering what I know
The point being
We know less about more

Nothing about everything
Everything about nothing
And in the end
Who knows?

Room with a view

In the heat of the day
Temperatures soaring
Safely nestled inside
My beautifully air-conditioned
Room with a view

Lucky beyond words
Swimming costume calling
Water inviting
Waiting for the shade
To cover the pool

Before the hot summer sun
Strays from the sky
Making way for the darkness
Of the long lonely night
And laying down to rest

Wandering and dementia

There has been a list of notices
And invitations to
Attend dementia seminars
'How to manage wandering'

It may be rather obvious soon
They are very annoying
Less than thoughtful
Very insulting

Although I may wonder
I am not a wanderer
Nor am I wandering
I am a person…

Sometimes people like to go for walks
Even people with dementia
Sometimes people get lost
Even people without dementia

Sometimes people go walking because they are bored
Even people with dementia
Sometimes people walk for exercise
Even people with dementia

We are Mothers Fathers Wives or Husbands
Daughters Sisters or Friends
We are not the labels
Of the symptoms of dementia

We are real people
With hearts and souls
Still able to feel the subtle
Lack of personhood

In the language that labels us
The words that insult
Continue to offend
And above all stigmatise us

Punched in the face

A new deficiency
Brought on by dementia
Forces us out of the denial bubble
Like a boxer in the ring

What is happening?
How can this be?
Surely things are OK?
The doctors are wrong?

Paddling so well
Like that damned calm swan
To hide the symptoms of dementia
No one sees the effort it takes

The paddling even fools us
Until my words are garbled
Or won't come out at all
And we are punched in the face again

Mrs Phillips and Mr Blair

She entered the shores of Australia
In search of change
And our cuddliest
Koala, Mr Blair

Gum leaves galore
But so much more
And nothing like
The other Mr Blair!

We teamed up
Hearts and spades within our reach
Creating opportunities
For dementia learning and transformation

In between hysterical laughing
And Master classes galore
Gumby and Pokey slightly bored
The Woodentops making up for it all

Definitely no longer imaginary friends
No axe murderers in sight
An @Saffy here an @Andrew there
And transformational respite

Why?

Why do we finish school?
Why do we search for that job we will love?
Or the next course we want to do
You know the one that will make all the difference…
Why does love lurch and loom in our lives?

Why do we seek peace and inner happiness?
The two things that seem to elude many of us
Why were we born in the first place,
When there are already so many people in the world?
Well, why not, you might think or say!

When your search for purpose
Turns into something truly beautiful
And more meaningful
Than you had dared to dream
This is why

Sadness

Sadness creeps into our souls
From our first breath
No warning
Never a choice

Sadness so stark
One can hardly speak
Barely a whisper
From a dry hoarse throat

Sadness to palpable
Like grit
Inside our eye sockets
Forcing us to tears

Sadness brought back
A piece of music
The waft of lavender
A place we might have shared

Sadness so overwhelming
We can only sit and cry
As if through obedience
Like a force from aliens

Sadness creating beauty
Lyrics poems and art
Stemming from the deep pit of sadness
Teaching us the deepest lessons on all

Balloons inside my head

My high functioning mind
Has slipped away
Sometimes showing itself like a ghost

Teasing me into believing
It will be okay
But now outside my reach

My thoughts fly around inside my head
Like helium balloons high inside an auditorium
Also out of reach

Memory and dinner plates

For the memory-impaired
Memory is like a stack of china
If you try to pull a plate from the middle
The whole thing comes crashing down

We need the time
To continue our stories
Chronologically and without interruption
One china plate at a time

Give us time to collect
What is left of our thoughts
And to find the words
To tell you about them

Resist the urge to give us a nudge
To hurry us along
As this is when
Our plates come crashing down

My disappearing world

Days alone with dementia
Laughter and love
Tragedy and sadness

Memory loss
Playing cards alone
Grief, tears, shock

Humiliation and stigma
Dancing
Daring

Keeping secrets
Engagement and inspiration
Hysterical and life changing

Lost in time

Moments lost in time
Remembering that once
I could cook a feast for thousands

The school reunions
Brimming with shared memories
A girlfriend's wedding fails to come to mind

Overseas holidays
No more than photos
Reminding me of where we've been

Moments lost in time
A feeling of emptiness
Paddling hard

It won't break my resolve
Working on new ways
And positive moments

To restore
The ever emptying shell
Harry's wand in high demand

Fighting off Dementors
Stealing my soul
And my disappearing world

Solitary tears

So many losses
Hidden from others
We must cry alone

So small yet so sad
Tragic incremental deaths
The jigsaw pieces of our lives

Dreams there one day
Gone the next
Fading like the light

Our stolen dreams
Healed through sharing
And the tears we shed alone

Vacant dements?

People with dementia
Are not 'vacant dements'
We are real human beings
Who still feel
And love

With the right to the same respect
The same autonomy
And privileges
Afforded to everyone
Without dementia

Be nice

Be nice
The simplest goal
On my list
Of great dreams

One for the celebrities
And sports people
As they speak out
To others

Oh, and a goal for the media
The neediest group of all
As they collectively
Slay those in their sights

No sign of niceness
Or respect for others
As they bang away at their computers
And talk into microphones

Be nice
The ultimate goal for people
Caring for those of us
Living with dementia

My garden

Inspiring me
To speak with more beauty
To be more beautiful

The weeds keeping life in balance
Reminding me
There is still work to be done

And after a spell of hot weather
Although it has been needy
It still showers me with its beauty

Think clearly

Transparency brings power
Clarity of thoughts produces results
When you know what you want, you can achieve it
Opportunities and events will appear…

To ensure you get out of life
What it is you truly want
It is up to you to think clearly

Add enthusiasm, patience and planning
To clarity and a sense of humour
Lots of hard work
And you will get where you plan to go

Go forth

Let the phrases in your books
Take you to places
More brilliant and evocative
Than any other journey

Don't let the sadness of dementia
Steal all of your dreams
Or stop you from reading
Stories of love

Read a book

Read with passion
Be open with your heart
Seek new ideas

Flourish amongst the words
Let them glow inside
And tease your brain

Online or on paper
Words bring life alive
With wonder

Be brave
Even if you forget
And read the same book!

Peace

If it is peace you want
Seek to change yourself
And not others

Truth

Truth has many faces
What appears to be a truth
Is usually a compromise
To accommodate different theories

What is your truth
Might be someone else's lie
What is my truth could well be as simple as
Something I've read in the newspaper!

Reactions to Mr Dementia

She 'came out' about the disease
Her son proclaimed
'But Mum, that's a funny old person's disease'
And with that they tried to laugh

Her mother felt anger
More than she had ever felt before
And then a desperate and deep sadness
That would not go away

Her husband worries when she's not looking
Waiting for another change
Another deficit to her abilities
As he watches her disappear

Some days he holds his head in his hands
Slouched on the bottom step
'I know I am losing you
And I am afraid of what the future holds'

Some friends disappear
Too afraid to face
The relentless changes
Brought on by Mr Dementia

Special friends

She held my heart gently in their hands
Beckoning me to face the sadness
No words or questioning
Simply sitting with love and friendship

This is what people with dementia need
More than anything else
Someone to hold their hearts lovingly
No one saying things like 'but I'm like that' or
'You don't have dementia'

And especially no blaming
The person who is changing
With the symptoms of
This very terminal disease

Letting go

As the symptoms of dementia
Force themselves upon me
I am forced to let go
Sometimes even ask for help

It makes me feel like vomiting
Giving up is not an option
What will happen to me and to us?
Will I turn into that empty shell?

Drowning

Some days it feels like I'm drowning
From the symptoms of dementia
No longer easy to stay afloat
Not a life saver in sight

As I start to sink
Towards the bottom
Of the crevice of dementia
My BUB no longer able to catch me

And no longer able
To paddle for myself
As the waves crash upon me
Pushing me further down

Paddling

Living with dementia
Looks like a swan
Calm on the surface

Paddling faster and harder
Below the surface
To stay afloat

Staying afloat

Staying afloat even though
The symptoms of dementia
Reach in and steal pieces of my soul

Too scared to stop paddling
Even for a minute to catch my breath
For fear I will sink

Swanning around

Calm and serene Swan
Paddling to stay afloat
Flapping her wings in the storm
But helpless to stop it

Maintaining dignity
Hiding humiliation
Wanting no one else to see
The ugly duckling on its way

Helpless

Helpless to stop the ugly duckling
That final stage of dementia
When no amount of flapping or paddling
Will overcome the confusion
Or the memory loss

Memory banking

Building up my memory bank
Blogging the words as fast as they appear
The feelings and insights of dementia

Helping me to feel less helpless
And others to understand
What the hell is happening to my brain

Who stole my soul?

Who the hell sucked out my soul?
Where did the Dementor come from?
Why did he appear?

Where is Harry with his wand?
Why won't he help?
Why won't he get rid of the damn Dementors?

Mr Dementia steals my soul
Like the bloody Dementors at Hogwarts
Who escaped from Azkaban

Helium balloons out of reach

My high functioning mind
Has slipped away
Sometimes showing itself like a ghost

Trying to tease me
Into believing it will be okay
But now outside of my reach

My thoughts fly around inside my head
Like helium balloons high inside an auditorium
Also out of my reach

The words escape me

Where do they go?
Those words I love
But cannot find

Slipped right back
Into the recesses
Of my brain

No longer in sight
Playing games
The words escape me

Love blown over

Love waits with open arms
Watches out for you
Stands still in the breeze

Sails through your heartstrings
Electrifying anticipation
The tempest of your heart

It blows over
You feel lost
Your love is in the wind

Love

Love so that you will never regret
Love so that you don't hurt others
Love so that you are free to grieve

Love so that you don't hurt yourself
Love without conditions
Love without boundaries

Love without borders of religion or race
Love with all the risk you would need
To fly to the moon on a broomstick

Life

Live your life
With honour
Shinier
And more beautiful
Than the brightest star

Loss

Loss
Leaves your heart searching
Your mind spinning
And a hole inside your soul

Loss
Leaves your heart feeling sad
Your mind numb
And an ache that darkens your soul

Loss
Leaves your heart blackened
Your mind empty of goals
And a blot on your soul

Loss
Leaves your heart mind and soul reeling
Whilst you find the path to healing
And then new love

Loss
Leaves you open to growth
And healing
And a deeper sense of meaning

Thank you

Two simple words
So often forgotten
Stalwarts of my youth
For fear of a tongue lashing

Seemingly less important
Today than then
But just as meaningful
And worthwhile

A smile and a thank you
Fills others' hearts with goodwill
Just add a bucket full of love
To complete the wonder

Love life and loss

Filled with kindness
Compassion and love
One seemingly empty brain
Can get through the day

With a flicker here
A faint glimmer there
Love life and loss
And days alone with dementia

The ups and downs of life

Nothing left to say
Other than I'm glad to be alive
And also realise,
You know it is love

When all you want
Is for that person to be happy
Even if you
Are not a part of their happiness

www.ingramcontent.com/pod-product-compliance
Lightning Source LLC
Chambersburg PA
CBHW062148100526
44589CB00014B/1736